BROTHER SONGS
A Male Anthology of Poetry

AUTUMN 1982

FOR MARK –

SOME MORE POETRY
. . . . .
FROM MOM

"I know that the spirit of God is the brother of my own,
And that all the men ever born are also my brothers . . ."
Walt Whitman
from *Song of Myself*

BROTHER SONGS

A Male Anthology of Poetry

Edited by Jim Perlman

HOLY COW! Press • MINNEAPOLIS • 1979

Library of Congress Cataloging in Publication Data
Main entry under title:

Brother Songs.

    1. American poetry—Men authors. 2. American
poetry—20th century. 3. Men—Poetry I. Perlman,
Jim, 1951— II. Title: A Male anthology of poems
about fathers, sons, brothers, friends, and lovers.

PS590.B7   811'.5'08   78-67028
ISBN 0-930100-02-6

Published by Holy Cow! Press
Post Office Box 618, Minneapolis, Minnesota 55440
Manufactured in the United States of America.

Cover design and all graphics by Randall W. Scholes

Typesetting by Morty Sklar's *The Spirit That Moves
Us* Press
Printing by McNaughton & Gunn, Lithographers
(Ann Arbor, Michigan)

Third Printing—Spring, 1981

Member: COSMEP, COSMEP-Midwest
Other titles from Holy Cow! Press:

letters to tomasito, Thomas McGrath. Twenty-three·
poems for and about the poet's son Tomasito. $2.00,
paper. (Second printing, 1979) 36 pages.

at the barre, Candyce Clayton. Poet's first published
collection. $2.50, perfectbound, 64 pages.

ACKNOWLEDGMENTS

Jon Anderson: "A Commitment" is reprinted from *In Sepia* by Jon Anderson by permission of the University of Pittsburgh Press. (c) 1974 by Jon Anderson.

Robert Bly: "Finding the Father" is reprinted from *This Body Is Made From Camphor and Gopherwood* by permission of Harper & Row, Publishers, Inc. (c) 1977 by Robert Bly.

Michael Dennis Browne: "Talk To Me, Baby" is reprinted from *The Sun Fetcher*, copyright (c) 1978 by Michael Dennis Browne and appears by permission of Carnegie-Mellon University Press. It first appeared in *The Iowa Review*.

Paul Carroll: "Father" is reprinted from *New and Selected Poems* by permission of Yellow Press. (c) 1978 by Paul Carroll.

Philip Dacey: "To the Poet's Father . . ." first appeared in *Poet & Critic* (Iowa State University, Ames, Iowa), Volume 5, Number 1.

James Dickey: "In the Tree House at Night" is reprinted from *Drowning With Others* by permission of Wesleyan University Press. Copyright (c) 1961 by James Dickey. The poem first appeared in *The New Yorker*.

Stephen Dunn: "After He Said" is reprinted from *A Circus of Needs* copyright (c) 1978 by Stephen Dunn and appears by permission of Carnegie-Mellon University Press.

David J. Feela: "Midnight Journey" first appeared in *Scribe* magazine.

Donald Hall: "My Son, My Executioner" is reprinted from *The Alligator Bride* copyright (c) 1969 by Donald Hall. By permission of Harper & Row, Publishers, Inc. It first appeared in *The New Yorker* (1954).

Robert Hutchinson: "My Brother's Braces" is reprinted from *Standing Still While Traffic Moved About Me*, Eakins Press, 1971. It first appeared in *Quarterly Review of Literature*, XI 2/3, 1962.

Ronald Koertge: "My Father" is reprinted from *The Father-Poems* (Sumac Press (c) 1973 by Ronald Koertge.

Ted Kooser: "Christmas Eve" first appeared in *The Nation*.

Norbert Krapf: "Cutting Wood: After a Family Photograph" is reprinted from *Finding the Grain* copyright (c) 1977 by Norbert Krapf. By permission of Dubois Co., Ind. Historical Society.

Philip Levine: "My Son and I" appeared in *Names of the Lost* (c) by Philip Levine, reprinted by permission of Atheneum Publishers. "You Can Have It" appeared in *Antaeus*, (c) 1978 by Philip Levine, by permission of *Antaeus*.

Gerald Locklin: "Son of Toad" is reprinted from *The Criminal Mentality* (c) by Gerald Locklin. By permission of Red Hill Press. It first appeared in *Wormwood Review*.

John Logan: "Poem For My Brother" first appeared in *Ironwood*. Reprinted by the kind permission of Michael Cuddihy and Ironwood Press.

Ken McCullough: "For Galway" is reprinted from *Creosote*, Seamark Press (c) 1976 by Ken McCullough. It first appeared in the *North Stone Review*.

Thomas McGrath: "Blues for Jimmy" is reprinted from *The Movie at the End of the World* (c) by Thomas McGrath. By permission of Swallow Press.

Ralph J. Mills, Jr.: "The Stones" first appeared in *Big Moon* (Spring, 1975). It's reprinted from *A Man to His Shadow* (c) 1975 by Ralph J. Mills, Jr. By permission of Juniper Press.

Steven Orlen: "Unwritten Letters" is reprinted from *Permission To Speak* by Steven Orlen. By permission of Wesleyan University Press (c) 1978. It first appeared in *Ironwood* and in the Ironwood Press chapbook, *Separate Creatures*.

Bill Pauly: "Heart/Song" is reprinted from *Into the Round Air*—an anthology published by Rook Press.

Robert Peters: "Night Regression Poem" is reprinted from *Cool Zebras of Light* (Christopher's Books, 1974). By permission of Robert Peters.

Carl Rakosi: "Song" is reprinted from *Ere-Voice* (c) 1971 by Carl Rakosi. By permission of Carl Rakosi.

George Roberts: "Andrew Talks To Gulls" first appeared in *North Stone Review*. It's reprinted from *The Blessing of Winter Rain* (Territorial Press).

Vern Rutsala: "The Furniture Factory" first appeared in *Harper's*.

Reg Saner: "Passing It On" is reprinted from *Climbing Into The Roots* (c) 1976 by Reg Saner. By permission of Harper & Row, Publishers, Inc.

Richard Shelton: "Letter to a Dead Father" is reprinted from *You Can't Have Everything* by Richard Shelton. By permission of the University of Pittsburgh Press (c) 1975 by Richard Shelton.

Morty Sklar: "Jarashow" is reprinted from *The Night We Stood Up For Our Rights* (c) 1977. By permission of Toothpaste Press. It first appeared in *The Actualist Anthology* (The Spirit That Moves Us Press, 1977).

Arthur Smith: "Carpenter" first appeared in *Rapport*, Volume 3, Number 2.

William Stafford: "My Father, His Friend, and Another" first appeared in *Kenyon Review*.

Gerald Stern: "The Hungarian" is reprinted from *Lucky Life* (c) 1977 by Gerald Stern. Reprinted by permission of Houghton Mifflin Publishers, Inc. It first appeared in *American Poetry Review*.

Charles Waterman: "To My Father" is reprinted from *Talking Animals* (c) 1977 by Charles Waterman. By permission of *Northeast*/Juniper Books.

David Wojahn: "Heaven for Railroad Men" first appeared in *CutBank*. Reprinted by permission of the editors.

Charles Wright: "Firstborn" is reprinted from *Hard Freight* by permission of Wesleyan University Press. Copyright (c) 1971 by Charles Wright. First appeared in *The Venice Notebook* (Barn Dream Press).

James Wright: "Two Postures Beside a Fire" (c) 1968 by James Wright. Reprinted from *Shall We Gather At The River* by permission of Wesleyan University Press.

This anthology is dedicated to:

My Mother and Father
   Grace & Everett C. Perlman

and in memory of my Grandmother
   Rose S. Feinberg (1885-1978)

Grateful thanks to Deborah Petersen and
Ronald Prieve for their help and to Don Eron,
Jim White, James Moore and David Wojahn for
their careful critical attention to these poems.

TABLE OF CONTENTS

III. Poems About Brothers

IV. Poems For Friends & Lovers

PREFACE

Several years ago, I attended a lecture — "The Evolution of Sexism in the English Language" — given by a self-described "radical-feminist-linguist." I was one of a handful of males in attendance and became convinced of how, in this society, language works to oppress all of us by the very connotations we've been trained to associate with words like "woman" and "man." It seems to be yet another example of how our patriarchal society holds us to roles by fitting us into conveniently labeled categories. I raised my hand . . . "but doesn't language also work to oppress *males*?" Yes, she agreed, and added "those males who question what it is to be a man are quickly whipped back into their places by other, more powerful males." It was an unsettling moment for me. Later, when I tried to seek out literature that addressed itself to this concept of "what it is to be a man," I was surprised to see how little writing exists that could be of help. Thus, the vague notion of collecting poems for an anthology began to take shape.

After two years of reading nearly 1,000 poems, *Brother Songs: A Male Anthology of Poetry*, came into being. I wanted to assemble a collection of poetry by contemporary American male poets that tried to confront this notion of "maleness" and how males relate to each other. I placed few limitations on the editing process other than wanting work from living poets and poems that weren't exclusively elegies (why do we wait for death to inspire us?). Was there writing that shattered traditional ideas of the male image and risked, among other things, displaying sensitive emotions? Indeed, *Brother Songs* seems to be a minority report in this regard. It seems that there are far too few of us who are willing to challenge the image of the unfeeling, competitive man. It's taboo, then, to want to express affection for other males, to cherish the life of a male child without a sticky-sweet sentimentality, to question the authority of fathers, or to risk a homosexual relationship. Notice that there are just a few poets here who even *dare* to break out of those expected, categorized relationships — perhaps they see that they are exploring the father-son-brother-friend potential within themselves!

Brother Songs, then, is not intended as a "definitive" anthology on the subject, but rather it should stand as part of a continuing exploration of these issues. Hopefully, this collection will serve as an inspiration for all of us.

Finally, I'd like to thank the hundreds of poets who were kind enough to send their work for consideration. I received work from every part of the country, by both well-known and relatively unknown poets who write with a wide range of styles and concerns. In many ways, it is to these poets that this anthology is dedicated.

Jim Perlman
Minneapolis—Iowa City
Spring, 1979

I. Poems About Fathers

FATHER'S TEAR.   1978   R.W. SCHOLES

FINDING THE FATHER

This body offers to carry us for nothing—as the ocean carries logs—so on some days the body wails with its great energy, it smashes up the boulders, lifting small crabs, that flow around the sides. Someone knocks on the door, we do not have time to dress. He wants us to come with him through the blowing and rainy streets, to the dark house. We will go there, the body says, and there find the father whom we have never met, who wandered in a snowstorm the night we were born, who then lost his memory, and has lived since longing for his child, whom he saw only once . . . while he worked as a shoemaker, as a cattle herder in Australia, as a restaurant cook who painted at night. When you light the lamp you will see him. He sits there behind the door . . . the eyebrows so heavy, the forehead so light . . . lonely in his whole body, waiting for you.

—Robert Bly

SAFELY

Every once in a while
I remember my father is alive
and it amazes me
because I have been living
as if I were alone in the world
without anyone to turn to
for advice or a lecture
and yet as to my father
aged and dry
what could he say to me
except that I also have to live
and die in my difficult time
except to show himself
in his brittle bones
as if to say,
I've had my day,
the lesson is to get to my condition
safely.

                    —*David Ignatow*

FATHER, HIS FRIEND, AND ANOTHER

Father's friend Ray at the planing mill
worked wood the color of afternoon air,
curls of it clasping everything there—
like the legs of the saw that mumbled at first,
and then the white shriek through birch.

While the two talked I felt the boards,
yellow and smooth, and uncurled rolls
of handshaved pine, put them like rings
around my arm to wear them home.
My father said, "Sure, leave them on."

As we started for home Father told me
that another man when they were all young
was close to them, and they sang in church.
When the other man died Ray ran out
to the country and hid, from grief—two days.

I remember that clutch, and I wave again
back through the sun at Father's friend.

—William Stafford

CUTTING WOOD: AFTER A FAMILY PHOTOGRAPH
(for my father)

The rickety steam engine clatters
in a frosted hollow of southern
Indiana hills. White puffs of steam
hang above a hedgerow of bare trees
in the background. You stand there,
grandfather, the ends of your moustache
curling about the corners of unsmiling
lips, grazing at the circular saw about
to bite into the green pulp of a log.
I feel in my blood your reverence
for the medium of wood, respect
your demand for the precise cut.

For twenty-five years your son
crafted processed wood into chairs.
He still stares at the grains
in wood. Now I, who remember touching
your hand only once before you died
in my third year, sit behind a desk
and daydream of the forests which
fed that saw. Soon after you lay
in the earth, your son led me into
the woods and cupped my ears to
the leafy murmurs of shagbark hickory,
wild cherry, oak and beech. He taught
me how to kill for food the animals
that ate on the fruits of those trees.

One short summer's work in a wood
factory still has me running my finger-
tips over the finished grain of woods
your rough saw once cut into lumber.
With your love of the precise cut,
grandfather, you would understand my
need to carve with a pen a line smooth
and delicate as wild cherry, yet tough
and durable as hickory. I glide over

8

the sawdust toward you, with the shadow
of the photographer caught in his picture.

—*Norbert Krapf*

A CHRISTMAS GIFT

This morning, father
handed me a gift
in a purple velvet case:
grandfather's tie pin.
Like grandfather's face
in the living room
picture, the metal
is a tarnished gold,
too tarnished to hold
the tie my neck won't wear.
Father said little;
all the directions
I've learned are settled
somewhere in my bones.

In 1903,
grandfather fled from
Japan's conscription.
What made him sail back
twenty years later
to arrange his bride
in flowerlike precision?
Then, near seventy,
why sail back once more,
this time to die? While
sunlight warms his grave,
five thousand miles
away I watch lights
on a pine flash on
and off in the dark:
red, blue, green and gold.

Often, years ago,
I'd wake in the night,
thinking that voices
were stirring in the house—
father, mother or
someone else—"David
has been . . . " *Been what?* I
asked before I fell
back asleep. Tonight,
father's foghorn snore

floats through the ceiling,
answering his father,
calling me to bed.
I listen one last time—
a child at Christmas.

—David Mura

CARPENTER

That winter, dark came early.
I remember halfway home
the leaves that murmured

in a red glow in the gutter,
the cold

whirring of the tablesaw
in the garage, my father
bent over frozen lumber
working.

While sun rays slanted
like ramps of yellow glass
up to the roof,

I was on my knees
piling the shavings,
gathering nails

and marbles of pine sap.
When he was done, high
on his shoulder
I went flying,

my ear brushing
the fluorescent lamp

that hummed against the rafters.
Into the warm house,
into the bright kitchen we went

where the smell of doughnuts
hung from the ceiling.

—Arthur Smith

FOR THE POET'S FATHER, ON HIS TAKING UP GARDENING LATE IN LIFE

What do you do among the tomato plants?
Tell me the same stories
you tell the roots and vines.

Here, after so long, you've learned to bury
each mistake, then take it weeks later
between your thumb and finger and break it off.

I am there, helmeted in green leaves,
and grow new,
a perfect specimen.
You eat your child clean
this time, and I am done,
but in my own heaven.

How did you know your memory
lay like good dirt in a backyard,
and would yield old faces,
words, deeds, each morning
like a cymbal crash,
only now leafed and in color,
made over like a new start?

Greet me as you greet them,
with your fingers framing a marvelous tale
of a short, happy life,
and I shall be all seed
and set myself
at many tables.

—Philip Dacey

TWO POSTURES BESIDE A FIRE

I.

Tonight I watch my father's hair,
As he sits dreaming near his stove.
Knowing my feather of despair,
He sent me an owl's plume for love,
Lest I not know, so I've come home.
Tonight Ohio, where I once
Hounded and cursed my loneliness,
Shows me my father, who broke stones,
Wrestled and mastered great machines,
And rests, shadowing his lovely face.

II.

Nobly his hands fold together in his repose.
He is proud of me, believing
I have done strong things among men and become a man
Of place among men of place in the large cities.
I will not waken him.
I have come home alone, without wife or child
To delight him. Awake, solitary and welcome,
I too sit near his stove, the lines
Of an ugly age scarring my face, and my hands
Twitch nervously about.

—James Wright

HEAVEN FOR RAILROAD MEN

You're still a young man,
he says, not to his son;
it's his bitterness
he's talking to
and at the restaurant
he orders a fourth round
before dinner,
with mother wiping her glasses
at the table, still believing
she's not going blind.

I help him from his chair
to the john. He pees slowly,
fingers like hams
on his fly, a complex
test of logic
for a man this drunk.
I'm splashing cold water on his face

and he tells me he's dying,
don't say a thing to your
mother and please, Dave,
don't ever remember me like this.

I remember how you said you
needed to
ride the baggage cars forever,
passing prairie towns
where silos squat like
pepper shakers on dry earth.
Father, I want to be six again
and sway with you

down the sagging rails
to Minot, Winnipeg, and beyond,
your mailsacks piled
like foothills of the Rockies.
You're unloading your government Colt,

unzipping your suitcase
for Canadian inspectors.
Father, when I touched you
I was trembling.

The heaven
of railroad men begins
with a collapsed trestle.
The engine goes steaming off
into nothing.
There are no rails to hold you,
you're singing country western
at the top of your lungs,
you go flying forever,
the door standing open,
sacks of mail scattering
like seed into space.

—David Wojahn

CHRISTMAS EVE

Now my father carries his old heart
in its basket of ribs
like a child coming into the room
with an injured bird.
Our ages sit down with a table between them,
eager to talk.
Our common bones are wrapped in new robes.
A common pulse tugs at the ropes
in the backs of our hands.
We are so much alike
we both weep at the end of his stories.

—Ted Kooser

THE FURNITURE FACTORY

Upstairs the sanders
rubbed fingernails
thin, hands shiny
and soft as a barber's—
men past forty
down on their luck.
Below, I worked in a haze
of fine dust
sifting down—
the lives of the sanders
sifting down, delicately
riding the cluttered
beams of light.
I pounded nails
on the line.
The wood swallowed hard
nailheads like coins
too thin to pick up.
Lunchtimes I read—
You gonna be
a lawyer, Ace?—
then forgot the alphabet
as I hammered
afternoons flat.
My father worked there too
breathing the sanding
room's haze.
We ate quiet lunches together
in the car.
In July
he quit—hands
soft, thick fingernails
feathery at the tips.

—*Vern Rutsala*✱

✱ HE TEACHES AT
LEWIS & CLARK

18

MY FATHER

lies on the same couch that he used to
only sit on, straight up as if the newsmen
might ask him to spring into action.

He used to work twelve hours a day making
ice cream from scratch. Then home, charging
around the lawn. Grass that had been mashed
flat he brought to attention then cut it off
at the roots, snuffing it out,
heartless.

He took one vacation, looking at the water in
Michigan with one eye, turning at every little
thing, each sound a customer. We dined at
roadside stands, covering six states in a week.
He ate standing, like a man on the run.

I saw him again last summer, four months past a
coronary. He rested in bed, gathering strength
for a nap, hands behind his head,
eyes full of ceilings.

—Ronald Koertge

VIGIL

When I was skiing
on the frozen Mississippi,
my father was swimming beside
the wide-eyed fishes
beneath my feet;
watching my steps
as they carried me past
a dormant moonlit farm
with an amber bulb
burning above
an open, broken porch.
The river bends with
arthritic joints in winter
but the power below
the frozen surface
is always there;
ice that lights
a thousand cities.
I cannot see him
or hear him
but I know he is swimming,
splashing,
tracing my tracks,
trying to understand
this midnight journey.

—*David J. Feela*

LETTER TO A DEAD FATHER

Five years since you died and I am
better than I was when you were living.
The years have not been wasted.
I have heard the harsh voices
of desert birds who cannot sing.
Sometimes I touched the membrane
between violence and desire
and watched it vibrate.
I learned that a man
who travels in circles
never arrives at exactly the same place.

If you could see me now
side-stepping triumph and disaster,
still waiting for you to say *my son*
my beloved son. If you could only see
me now, you would know I am stronger.

Death was the poorest subterfuge
you ever managed, but it was permanent.
Do you see now that fathers
who cannot love their sons
have sons who cannot love?
It was not your fault
and it was not mine. I needed
your love but I recovered without it.
Now I no longer need anything.

— Richard Shelton

JARASHOW

Ancient store of olden time
on Jamaica Avenue . . .

Old woman
   in black shawl
      zinc grey hair
     & grey face:
          "I remember you, you were six
        when you came around
        with your father."

(Yes, Mrs. J
   I don't remember you
but I've been here
   somewhere

   The dust which
  should be dirt and filth
   isn't, in your place
           it's piled
      upon layer after year,
        and inventories
     nor windy doors disturb or mingle.

Handtruck up-
on which I throw cartons
of tools
   for that black and dusty place
     highceilinged of pressed tin

       steel drawers
a hundred sizes   thousands of nuts bolts & screws
         pipes   fittings & nails . . .

On 160th & 91st Avenue
a block from the old Jamaica El,
   unloading a '70 Chevy

to a worn handtruck,
motions are fast
like my father's
but not because the cartons are future,
pieces of my life. yet
they feel that way,
his blood is in them.

Driving back
    thru Union Turnpike towns past Utopia
        Pk'way homes, I speak to Dad
    in my head: Mrs. Jarashow remembers me;
        I told her you mean my brother she said
            "no, you were six
        when you came around with your father . . ."
I feel he'll be pleased
because what's happened since
is over
                    there's time
                    to finish the circle,
                    talk with my father
                    who began it heading a fatherless
                    brood,
                            rushing
                                    til now.

I being wellfed
                had gone another way
        blessd it comes to this
        as in old times
        when sons came home.
    Once, Home was a direction Thatway,
        now it's where I am, my father's house
            is one place.

When Jarashow's was new
    with maple counters and zinc boxes,
    when a young man with his woman

23

stood in the doorway

  my father was selling hardware & tools
from joblots, boxes and Grandpa's cellar . . .
  at 35 he'd made mistakes,
    was starting out again,
  he

who hustled in the streets
    of Jersey City, downtown Manhattan,
  Astoria
      my father who (he never let on til *I*
        did it) took chances,
      made a bundle in woolens on daring,
      lost, bought a barrel of peanuts
      and peddled them
      from a furnished room.

Father, see,
  I too have aimed
  for what I want
  —a little late and unsure,
  but now it's the same.
  I won't wait
  for graveside poems—
  there's time before Kaddish
    and everything's okay
    between you and me.

                    —*Morty Sklar*
                    1970

24

FATHER

How sick
I get of your ghost.
And of always looking at this tintype on my desk
of you as a cocky kid:
Kilkenney's coast, rocks and suncracked turf
giving the resilience to your countenance
as you try to seem so nonchalant, posing
in a rented Sunday morning suit,
spats and bowler hat:
a greenhorn off the boat. And yet,
something in that twist of fist,
knuckles taut about the cane knob, shows
how you already seem to know
you'll transform that old cow pasture of Hyde Park
into your own oyster.

The way you did.

And that other photo
stuck somewhere in my dresser
drawer
amid the Xmas handkerchiefs
the rubbers, poems
and busted rosary beads:
Posed beneath three palmtrees
on Tampa Beach's boardwalk,
a stocky man who'd made his millions by himself;
and could quarrel with Congressmen in Washington
about the New Deal bank acts;
or call Mayor Kelly crooked to his face.

Hair,
bone, cock,
face and skin, brains:
rotten in the earth these 16 years.

Remember, father, how Monsignor Shannon
(whose mouth you always said

25

looked exactly like a turkey's ass)
boomed out Latin above your coffin at Mount Olivet?
But as the raw October rain
rasped against our limousine
guiding the creeping cars back into
Chicago,
Jack, your first born,
picked his nose; and
for an instant flicked a look
to ask if I too knew you were dead for good—
St Patrick's paradise a club
for priests and politicians
you wouldn't get caught dead in.

You used to like to call me Bill.
And kiss me. Take me to the Brookfield Zoo.
Or stuff English toffee in my mouth.
But always after you'd cursed
and with a bedroom slipper
whacked the tar out of Jack.

This morning, father,
broke as usual,
no woman in my bed,
I threw six bucks away
for a shave and haircut at The Drake.
And looked again for you.
On Oak Street beach,
gazing beyond the bathers and the boats,
I suddenly searched the horizon, father,
for that old snapshot of Picasso
and his woman Dora Maar.
Picasso bald and 60;
but both in exaltation, emerging
with incredible sexual dignity
from the waters of the Gulfe Juan.

Tattoo
of light

26

on lake.

Bleached spine of fish.

Those ripples of foam: semen of the ghost.

I left the lake;
but tripped in the quick dark
of the Division Street underpass;
then picked a way past newspaper scraps,
puddles and a puckered beachball.
I looked for dirty drawings on the wall.
Traffic crunches overhead.
This underpass is endless.

—Paul Carroll

FATHER

it is hard not feeling you inside me
for all those years you were so distant
feeling the new country take shape in you
trying to caress even the thorns on the gentile Christ

I live with you every day
but then I believed you weren't inside me
I know I wanted to be something else
some farmer of words in my desert
I remember one day when we went camping
you laughed you wanted to do something for me
"to my dear son" this book I didn't read for years
after you gave it to me

you were so distant when I was young
I wanted you next to me at night
so I could fall asleep on your lap
and you would carry me to bed half asleep
and I would dream and dream till morning

you were so good to me but so distant afraid
an immigrant afraid of the world
needing an enemy to live
to live on in you to define yourself
you took up painting to love something in yourself

I wondered if you loved your children
even when you worked hard for them
were you able to say what you really wanted to hear
your misery and your joy your fears the shadow
no one to listen the need to define it yourself

of all the years we were together
I hardly remember a moment
all of it is empty empty of your embrace
and I cry and cry for the loss for I am your loss
I am what became of you ashamed and slightly proud

inhibited with laughter afraid
of being alone of not being heard
afraid I won't like myself
remembering the fear of death in my grandmother's eyes
not peaceful but frantic
half ripened in the wrong oven
with only memories of another life

I want to understand what remains of you in myself
if only to forgive you for what I could not undo
and our ancestors we both carry with us
the dark shadows flow into the ground
when evening comes they are everywhere
no longer a ghost no longer a memory of wandering
permanent at night the look of the Jews

my father it is enough to look at you in your old age
to know how I wanted to be loved
this aching hole which is a mouth in the earth
where we are buried with your sorrows but still speak
father I don't want to curse myself or my luck
I am here living each day with myself
putting my voice out to feel around
to laugh to smooth out the tired muscles
to be foolish to be extravagant in love
to awaken with the sun on my naked body
and my wife at my side and my dear son next to us
peaceful in bones and glance and voice and laughter

I am moving away from you now to warm a cold place
to burn off my awkwardness with my live heart
to know myself and my son and my wife each moment
and follow the eyes of the day across the sky
and the moon at night with its scars of change
I am going away to discover what I do not know of myself
and stop pretending my fingers are frozen at the waistline of my voice
all these years somehow seemingly wasted
the relatives who do not speak the friends dispersed
the love and comfort unreturned the life to be made and made again

you grew up short five feet one from the ground
looking up at the new land you came to many years ago
your mother leaving you your father gone
who comforted you whom did you feel you could love
securely at night who read to you was quiet with you
who walked by your side who gave you his smile your own
and I cried for you as you cried watching the moon
as tears fell and fell and the darkness fell around you
I remembered reading *Call it Sleep* and there you were in that book
and I cried and cried for what I wanted from you and never got
and now I am on my own repeating your sorrow
but washing it away with my own tears not with other's
I do not know which way to go because there is nowhere to go
and yet I am leaving leaving with the moon at my back
and am happy to be going so far away
not for escape but for adventure
and each moment the adventure of what is happening
clearly and unreservedly I will not look only at parts

I want to say good-bye properly but I don't know how
perhaps when the time comes I will find the way
it is hard to be strong but I am strong
stronger than you have made me

—*Sid Gershgoren*

PASSING IT ON

I was three and already
my world shook with you.
Now I'm what's left. The eyes
I have are yours, your mouth.
That trick of your upper lip—
and those slurred l-syllables
you still slide
into a few of my words.

Now in my dreams again
and again your lacquered
casket sinks, becomes your door
into the grass. To one side
the clay heap waits to fall
a shovelful at a time.

I walk up close. I heft a clod,
then eat. Gnawing, I taste
the darkness between us
you suddenly died in. For years
it's been the red fist
of your heart that I've chewed
and gagged on, till I'm bled out
and odd of it.

And your small, thick hands.
Their anger has made my own hand
tremble, passing it on.

Already I'm hurt
by my son's look—the way
his eyes beat and grow secret
under this strange love
shaken into me.

                        —*Reg Saner*

II. Poems For Sons

SON, GROWIN' UP TOMATERS.   1978   R.W. SCHOLES

FIRSTBORN

—Omnia quae sunt, lumina sunt—

1

The sugar dripping into your vein;
The jaundice rising upon your face like a blush;
The glass box they keep you in—

The bandage over your eyes;
The curdled milk on your lips;
The plastic tube in your throat—

The unseen hands that linger against your skin;
The name, like a new scar, at your wrist;
The glass box they keep you in—

We bring what we have to bring;
We give what we have to give:
Welcome, sweet Luke, to your life.

2

The bougainvillaea's redress
Pulses throughout the hillside, its slow
Network of vines

Holding the earth together, giving it breath;
Outside your window, hibiscus and columbine
Tend to their various needs;

The summer enlarges.
                    You, too, enlarge,
Becoming accessible,
Your liquid reshufflings

Protracted and ill defined,
Yet absolute after all, the new skin
Blossoming pink and clear.

3

You lie here beside me now,

35

Ineffable, elsewhere still.
What should one say to a son?

Emotions and points of view, the large
Abstractions we like to think
We live by—or would live by if things

Were other than what they are;
Or we were; or others were;
If all were altered and more distinct?

Or something immediate,
Descriptive, the virtuous use of words?
What can one say to a son?

4
If it were possible, if
A way had been overlooked
To pull that rib of pure light

Out of its cage, those few felicitous vowels
Which expiate everything . . .
But nothing has been left out,

Nothing been overlooked.
The words remain in the dark, and will
Continue to glitter there;

No tricks we try to invent,
No strategies, can now extract them.
And dust is dust for a long time.

5
What I am trying to say
Is this—I tell you, only, the thing
That I have come to believe:

Indenture yourself to the land;
Imagine you touch its raw edges

In all weather, time and again;

Imagine its colors; try
To imitate, day by day,
The morning's growth and the dusk,

The movement of all their creatures;
Surrender yourself, and be glad;
This is the law that endures.

6
The foothills of Tennessee,
The mountains of North Carolina,
Their rivers and villages

—Hiwassee and Cherokee,
The Cumberland, Pisgah and Nantahala,
Unaka and Unicoi—

Brindle and sing in your blood;
Their sounds are the sounds you hear,
Their shapes are the shapes you see

Regardless, whenever you concentrate
Upon the remembered earth
—All things that are are lights.

—*Charles Wright*

FOR GALWAY
(born Feb. 16, 1971)

Lying in the middle of our bed
    covers up to your double chin
you look
    like a handsome toad
sunning on some princess's pillow.

Your winter hair
    slips from its follicles;
I listen
    at the ripe pulse of your fontanel
    healing the split of existence itself

and my own drunk membranes
spasm at the
    voice
    yodeling me back into darkness.

As the sky
    opens its nocturnal bloom
high in the eaves
    of the solemn conifers
I write this, my son,
    your Easter poem —
making
    obeisance to Ishtar, the widow
    of shadows
your Mother, mine
the Goddess beneath our four awkward feet
obeisance to Christ-child
    child in eternity —
eternity;
    eternal word of the uninspired.
Thus I use it, in full
    knowledge of my state.

I pray on this, your fifty-fourth day
that we may find a way to help you
    be this child forever;
to be afraid of the darkness —

not afraid, but apprehensive;

Regard it as a mystery
        my aquarian miracle
and learn to move through it
as a virgin priest, for the first time
        in the nimble pack of fingers
        —of woman—

Sleep
        in the folds of light.

                        —*Ken McCullough*

THE MILKY WAY

When I was a boy, the Milky Way
      Floated just over the City
Of Boston, so I was lucky to live
      In that place, that
House where my father lathered
      His face & like the moon
Went out, came back, walking
      Winter nights beneath
The Milky Way. Few thoughts,
      Few fears, a way of
Sleeping through the night.

      When my son lay sewn
To the sheets, adrift in his
      Diabetic coma among
The blown, seductive stars,
      I could not think of
Anything to say, for he was
      Not anywhere nearby.
So he said *Pa-Pa* and came back.
      Tonight, in his play,
He captains a sleek star ship
      Toward the Milky Way.

When I was a boy, the City of
      Boston lay miles away
Within our sight. Evenings we
      Set our chairs upon
The lawn and talked. Few thoughts,
      A way of watching until
Dark. Then as our small wickers
      Floated through the night
I wished I might be taken away
      To live forever in that
Distant city made wholly of light.

—*Jon Anderson*

40

FOR MY SON NOAH, TEN YEARS OLD

Night and day arrive, and day after day goes by,
and what is old remains old, and what is young remains young, and
      grows old,
and the lumber pile does not grow younger, nor the weathered two by
      fours lose their darkness,
but the old tree goes on, the barn stands without help so many years,
the advocate of darkness and night is not lost.

The horse swings around on one leg, steps, and turns,
the chicken flapping claws onto the roost, its wings whelping and
      whalloping,
but what is primitive is not to be shot out into the night and the dark.
And slowly the kind man comes closer, loses his rage, sits down at
      table.

So I am proud only of those days that we pass in undivided tenderness,
when you sit drawing, or making books, stapled, with messages to
      the world. . .
or coloring a man with fire coming out of his hair.
Or we sit at a table, with small tea carefully poured;
so we pass our time together, calm and delighted.

—Robert Bly

MY SON, MY EXECUTIONER

My son, my executioner,
  I take you in my arms,
Quiet and small and just astir,
  And whom my body warms.

Sweet death, small son, our instrument
  Of immortality,
Your cries and hungers document
  Our bodily decay.

We twenty-five and twenty-two,
  Who seemed to live forever,
Observe enduring life in you
  And start to die together.

—Donald Hall

HEART/SONG FOR CHRISTOPHER RAYMOND

Zero night
for leaving,
son,
mariner

on wish-
bone chip
of moon
sailing home.

Christopher,
be well compassing
oceandark
your birth day hymn,

star storm
in the eye.
We sail, too.
Still. Born.

    —Bill Pauly

TO MY FATHER

Now I have a son. I see
when he grows sleepy
and, inside his round, fierce head,
are unaccountable games of love,
whole towns
such as we are from.
He needn't fear them,
and of course he doesn't;
he merely looks
at the beings in the fire
and understands how
they go under,
and how they arise.
He makes us study with him,
makes us philosophize.
Who is the child, now?
He teases us both toward love
and makes us laugh.

                    —*Charles Waterman*

GRAHAM

my dear son whom I put to bed each evening
I am almost frantic with love for you
I see you growing out of my darkening hands
as each year opens you more and more
I yearn for a souvenir of you
a little son in my breast
I remember how you came into
the soft light
and were held by it
and now I know the way
you say words
tiny words
little grey horses
come out of your mouth
your room with so many upright things
that fall asleep at attention
remains with you
gathered into your sleep
you eat
dreaming of how your muscles felt
when the wind you couldn't see
strapped itself around you
and you have no patience
for what may come to you
rising from the voice
crickets
minted in your ear
the moon half full going down with you
captain of the ocean of your sleep
I wrap my fog of love around you
imagining you in the other boys I meet
their wild eyes burning
in the center of the rock
that hits the crow
and I am ageless with you around me
by the river I walked as by the edge of my vision
I saw you appear from the bend for an instant
appear in and out of time

the stones around sacred places were meant to preserve you
now you sometimes go to bed yourself

—*Sid Gershgoren*

HEARING MY SON PLAY

handsomely into his instrument his door he
you hear him enter you sense
this antecedent of sorrow
a quiet an almost invisible presence

the violin is a smile that has yet to awaken
(you and I my son we two are rivers)
and he waits
poised over the icy glockenspiel of the world

the room is a place we have all known in dream
how the mist surrounds makes islands out of mountains
cold dawns of inaudible heartbeat
and he begins warms his fingers over a first frugal melody
pulls his hands out of a magic carton of hunger
they breakfast on dance
that disciplined gentle rage of Bach

you know where it takes us
music has always wanted us free
our eyes have often told us earth is beautiful
and I listen
you
in white
unfold unknowable sunlight

the mountain is residence elevation
(that is why your Brahms sounds so pure)
roosters axes and axles
clouds
the lowing of wool
wind
abyss
water and light embracing in thunder

you invent patience and perfume
your black friend plays his harmonium

47

a girl behind you sustains an arpeggio
together you improvise
touching the body of India

so you see
whatever you do
has the unconveyable sweetness of prayer
I remember your smallness in your mother's arms
it was the smallness of an instrument
that would grow out of bounds

—*Alvaro Cardona-Hine*

SON OF TOAD

someone recently asked my kid,
john william (kubla) locklin,
what he wants to be when he grows up.
he said, "a toad."

naturally i was thrilled as any father
whose son aspires to follow in his steps.

here, then, my boy, is what you may look forward to:
an onanistic adolescence,
a promising but brief young manhood,
consummating in a steep descent into obesity,
declining powers, and the nether twilight
this side of oblivion.

son, i would like to spare you this,
but another of the toad-conditions
is the forfeiture of the capacity
to alleviate the destiny of one's loved ones.

what's more, all that is offered in compensation
is the chance that an occasional young girl
or literary magazine will find insensitivity refreshing.

think it over, my beautiful and innocent young john-john:
wouldn't you prefer to be the eagle, lion, or the shark?

if, however, your mind is irrevocably set,
accept this charge: you must always wear
the verdant mantle with a wry hauteur . . .
and never reveal the secret of making love toad-style.

—Gerald Locklin

OUT-AND-DOWN PATTERN

My young son pushes a football into my stomach
and tells me that he is going to run
an out-and-down pattern,
and before I can check the signals
already he is half way across the front lawn,
approaching the year-old mountain ash,
and I turn the football slowly in my hands,
my fingers like tentacles
exploring the seams,
searching out the lacing,
and by the time I have the ball positioned
just so against the grain-tight leather,
he has made his cut downfield
and is now well beyond the mountain ash,
approaching the linden,
and I pump my arm once, then once again,
and let fire.

The ball in a high arc
rises up and out and over the linden,
up and out over the figure
that has now crossed the street,
that is now all the way to Leighton Avenue,
now far beyond,
the arms outstretched,
the head as I remember it
turned back, as I remember it
the small voice calling.

And the ball at the height of its high arc
begins now to drift,
to float as if weightless
atop the streetlights and the trees,
becoming at last that first bright star in the west.

Late into an early morning
I stand on the front porch,
looking into my hands.

My son is gone.

The berries on the mountain ash
are bursting red this year,
and on the linden
blossoms spread like children.

—*William Kloefkorn*

PLANTING

The years seem to tumble
faster and faster
I work harder;
the boys are larger;
we planted apple and cherry.

       in summer, barefoot,
in winter, rubber boots.

Little boys bodies
soft bellies, tiny nipples,
dirty hands.

New grass coming
thru oakleaf and pine needle —
I'll plant a few more trees,
then watch
the slow sky turn.

            —Gary Snyder

ANDREW TALKS TO GULLS

for my son

standing on a string of grey rocks
reaching out into the clear water
andrew talks to gulls

his voice   sliding through octave cries
light as time   lifts in clouds of gulls
and draws their tiny black eyes

he thinks those pure white birds come
out of the sky and across years of water
for the pieces of bread he scatters to them

i know the sun dancing on their yellow beaks
is in honor of this small boy
whose voice remembers

he too   once wore
white feathers

—George Roberts

SAUNDERS POINT

The Niantic River pauses
in a change of tides.
Wind skims the water,
a pattern I've seen
wind make over tall grass.
My son will not follow me back
to our house. He fears the storm less
than the bloated face of a thunderhead
in his children's book.
I must tell him
what he already knows.
His mother will soon die.
I have to explain "forever"
to my three-year-old son, Sam.
He is tilting his head
to a sound I can't hear
between the claps of thunder.
I imagine he senses
a kind of motion
where future lives are possible
in the past. But Sam lives
with his whole heart in the present.
I'd trade any brains I have
to feel the inexhaustible joy
he feels pushing his feet
into the wet sand
which circles dry around each foot.

—*Henry Combellick*

MY SON AND I

In a coffee house at 3 am
and he believes
I'm dying. Outside the wind
moves along the streets
of New York City picking up
abandoned scraps of newspapers
and tiny messages of hope
no one hears. He's dressed
in worn corduroy pants
and shirts over shirts,
and his hands are stained
as mine once were
with glue, ink, paint.
A brown stocking cap
hides the thick blond hair
so unlike mine. For forty
minutes he's tried not
to cry. How are his brothers?
I tell him I don't know,
they have grown away
from me. We are Americans
and never touch on this
stunned earth where a boy
sees his life fly past
through a car window. His mother?
She is deaf and works
in the earth for days, hearing
the dirt pray and guiding
the worm to its feasts. Why
do I have to die? Why
do I have to sit before him
no longer his father, only
a man? Because the given
must be taken, because
we hunger before we eat,
because each small spark
must turn to darkness.
As we said when we were kids
and knew the names of everything
. . . just because. I reach
across the table and take

55

his left hand in mine.
I have no blessing. I can
tell him how I found
the plum blossom before
I was thirty, how once
in a rooming house in Alicante
a man younger than I,
an Argentine I barely understood,
sat by me through the night
while my boy Teddy cried out
for help, and how when he slept
at last, my friend wept
with thanks in the cold night.
I can tell him that his hand
sweating in mine can raise
the Lord God of Stones,
bring down the Republic of Lies,
and hold a spoon. Instead
I say it's late, and he pays
and leads me back
through the empty streets
to the Earl Hotel, where
the room sours with the mould
of old Bibles dumped down
the air-shaft. In my coat
I stand alone in the dark
waiting for something
a flash of light, a song,
a remembered sweetness
from all the lives I've lost.
Next door the TV babbles
on and on, and I give up
and sway toward the bed
in a last chant before dawn.

—*Philip Levine*

III. Poems About Brothers

BROTHER ON HORN LADDER.   1978   R. W. SCHOLES

POEM FOR MY BROTHER

Blue's my older brother's color. Mine is brown, you see.
So today I bought this ring
of gold and lapis lazuli flecked with bright bronze.
His blue is the light hue of his eyes. Brown's the color
of our dead mother's long hair,
which fell so beautifully about her long shoulders
in the picture, and of my own eyes (I can't tell hers).
I loved my brother, but never knew quite what to think.
For example, he would beat
me up as soon as the folks
left the house, and I would cry big, loud feminine tears.
He was good at sports and played football, and so instead
I was in the marching band.
My brother stole rubbers from the store and smoked cigars
and pipes, which made me sick. But
once we swam together in
the Nishnabotna river
near home, naked, our blue overalls piled together
by the water, their copper
buttons like the bronze glints in my ring. I remember
once when I was very young
I looked deep into a pool
of blue water—we had no mirror—and I was so
amazed I looked over my shoulder, for I did not
imagine it was me, caught
in that cerulean sky.
Thinking it was someone other, I tell you I con-
fused myself with my brother!
Nothing goes with gold, but I can see in this rich blue
stone the meeting of our clothes like the touching of hands
when he taught me to hold my fishing pole well and wound
up the reel for me. You know
blue's the last of the primary colors to be named.
Why, some primitive societies still have no word
for it except "dark." It's associated with black:
in the night brother and I
would play at games that neither of us could understand.
But this is not a confession; it is a question.

We've moved apart and don't write,
and our children don't even know their own cousin!
So, I would have you know I
want this ring to *engage* us
in reconciliation.
Blue's the color of the heart.
I won't live forever. Is it too late now to be
a brother to my brother?
Let the golden snake bend round
again to touch itself and
all at once burst into azure!

—John Logan

"BEYOND THE WINDOW"

beyond the window
night, spacious and
warm, wine dark,
sounds full and distant,
some faint sensation
exhumed of darkness.
it is autumn, our
house stilled save
for the slow settling
of age, and here, next
to you, my brother, in
the bed once shared by
our parents i lie taut
for fear of sounding
the great springs anxious
with rust which wake
the sleepers beneath us.
dream has shaken me:
a great terror-shadow
invades our room, its
dark extensions sleep
lurching toward us.
wild with fear, our
angular bodies draw near
deep within our blanketed
hovel, and our mouths,
with a great
gaping silence, tremble.
then, sudden sharp
sense of a fall
shakes me, this
and a child-cry
or moan sounding
of a distance drawn
between us. now, my
nose nuzzled in
sheet and pillow, catches
the fading odor
of our stilled boy-
bodies mingling warm
beneath the covers, and

i fear its passing.
indefinite in this night,
you are a shadow form
beside me in silence,
and to settle the
distance of that silence
is why now, you are
startled by a young
arm heavy on your
subtle shoulder.

—*Joseph P. Darcy*

IN THE TREE HOUSE AT NIGHT

And now the green household is dark.
The half-moon completely is shining
On the earth-lighted tops of the trees.
To be dead, a house must be still.
The floor and the walls wave me slowly;
I am deep in them over my head.
The needles and pine cones about me

Are full of small birds at their roundest,
Their fists without mercy gripping
Hard down through the tree to the roots
To sing back at light when they feel it.
We lie here like angels in bodies,
My brothers and I, one dead,
The other asleep from much living,

In mid-air huddled beside me.
Dark climbed to us here as we climbed
Up the nails I have hammered all day
Through the sprained, comic rungs of the ladder
Of broom handles, crate slats, and laths
Foot by foot up the trunk to the branches
Where we came out at last over lakes

Of leaves, of fields disencumbered of earth
That move with the moves of the spirit.
Each nail that sustains us I set here;
Each nail in the house is now steadied
By my dead brother's huge, freckled hand.
Through the years, he has pointed his hammer
Up into these limbs, and told us

That we must ascend, and all lie here.
Step after step he has brought me,
Embracing the trunk as his body,
Shaking its limbs with my heartbeat,
Till the pine cones danced without wind

65

And fell from the branches like apples.
In the arm-slender forks of our dwelling

I breathe my live brother's light hair.
The blanket around us becomes
As solid as stone, and it sways,
With all my heart, I close
The blue, timeless eye of my mind.
Wind springs, as my dead brother smiles
And touches the tree at the root;

A shudder of joy runs up
The trunk; the needles tingle;
One bird uncontrollably cries.
The wind changes round, and I stir
Within another's life. Whose life?
Who is dead? Whose presence is living?
When may I fall strangely to earth,

Who am nailed to this branch by a spirit?
Can two bodies make up a third?
To sing, must I feel the world's light?
My green, graceful bones fill the air
With sleeping birds. Alone, alone
And with them I move gently.
I move at the heart of the world.

—*James Dickey*

IN MY BROTHER'S HOUSE

for Leonard

Until the age of five
my hair was blond.
Then it changed,
darkened, as though
a cloud had settled
just above my head

to stay. My brother
understands me
at times so well
I can see myself
running to hide
in his mouth when

he is silent. I
remember the attic
we would go to
as children; we knew
that there the secrets
of the house

revealed themselves,
and there, we too
could be understood.
Secretly, we
would pluck one wire
on the inside

of the dusty, ragged
piano, and that note
spread, circled us
as though we were
a fire, around which
the ritual of love

was being performed.
Under the naked beams
we listened and
listened. It was a life
rising, a life settling.
And now, unlucky in love,

I have come to talk
with my brother, and
before he says a word,
in the quiet as he hands
me a drink of bourbon,
I hear that note

again and feel at home.

—*Mick Fedullo*

YOU CAN HAVE IT

My brother comes home from work
and climbs the stairs to our room.
I can hear the bed groan and his shoes drop
one by one. You can have it, he says.

The moonlight streams in the window
and his unshaven face is whitened
like the face of the moon. He will sleep
long after noon and waken to find me gone.

Thirty years will pass before I remember
that moment when suddenly I knew each man
has one brother who dies when he sleeps
and sleeps when he rises to face this life,

and that together they are only one man
sharing a heart that always labors, hands
yellowed and cracked, a mouth that gasps
for breath and asks, Am I gonna make it?

All night at the ice plant he had fed
the chute its silvery blocks, and then I
stacked cases of orange soda for the children
of Kentucky, one gray boxcar at a time

with always two more waiting. We were twenty
for such a short time and always in
the wrong clothes, crusted with dirt
and sweat. I think now we were never twenty.

In 1948 in the city of Detroit, founded
by de la Mothe Cadillac for the distant purposes
of Henry Ford, no one wakened or died,
no one walked the streets or stoked a furnace,

for there was no such year, and now
that year has fallen off all the old newspapers,

calendars, doctors' appointments, bonds,
wedding certificates, drivers licenses.

The city slept. The snow turned to ice.
The ice to standing pools or rivers
racing in the gutters. Then bright grass rose
between the thousands of cracked squares,

and that grass died. I give you back 1948.
I give you all the years from then
to the coming one. Give me back the moon
with its frail light falling across a face.

Give me back my young brother, hard
and furious, with wide shoulders and a curse
for God and burning eyes that look upon
all creation and say, You can have it.

—Philip Levine

THE RIVER KLEEG

And we went there.

Q. Why?
A. Because we were young
and the water boiled up
over the rocks
and there was a grassy spot
to take a girl
or eat a bologna sandwich
hard boiled egg.

Q. And you were happy?
A. Happy. Well we were involved.
The hands reached out
the branch was there
the sky was blue
we lived in a cool breeze
of the inevitable.
"Gift" was the shouting
of each bird.

Q. What happened? Describe a trip.
A. Typically there were two of us.
My brother and I.
He did what I could not.
I did the rest.
He made the eggs.
I cut the wood.
He rowed the boat.
I caught the fish.
But we both laughed.

Q. And you were not touched?
A. Oh I think it was the sun smiled.
And everywhere we went
was our address.

I slept not one bad night
with even the rocks under me
With even the snows, the rain.
It seemed we were the children
of the snow, the rain.
If what you mean by touch
is were we hurt
I tell you there was once
I stopped to get my breath
on a long climb up a hill
Jeff knew.
I reached out for that breath
and it was there.

Q. It seems then things were good?
A. It seems then things were good.
    The grim catastrophe tomorrow would become
    had not yet turned its headlines
    in my heart.
    I said, if only to the wind,
    I am alive!
    And pitied everyone not in my shoes.
    My brother—who knows what he lived.
    But I was safe.

Q. What was the river like, the River Kleeg?
A. There was a turbulence in spots.
    There were big rocks, and
    pools behind that looked like maple syrup.
    One night a hatch of flies
    came off the flats.
    I lit a cigarette
    beside a tree,
    pissed on some lichens
    near the trail
    watching the steam rise.
    Among the overhang of branches
    near the stream

we built the fire
nestled in among the stones.
It snapped in the night air
from the sapped wood
we fed it.
Oh it talked, we let it.
We let it do all the talking.

Q. Do you think, if I could get time off
    in the spring, you could take me there.
A. It would be good to go there once again.
    But oh, dear friend, the way is lost.

                        —*Greg Kuzma*

TALK TO ME, BABY

1

A friend at a cocktail party tells me
of being on a fishing trip up North
and meeting some men from Illinois
who showed him how to clean and filet a fish properly;
and of how, when one particular pike
was stripped almost clean, almost all of him gone,
the jaw with the razory teeth opened
and some kind of cry came from the creature,
that head on the end of almost no body;
and the man with the knife said:
"Talk to me, baby."

2

Up in the Boundary Waters last weekend
I hooked a trout, my first, and played him.
I got him to the shallows
and tried to raise him. And the girls
got down into the water with my leather hat—
we hadn't brought a net—and I was yelling
"I've got a fish! I've got a fish!"
out into the evening, and the girls
tried to get him into the hat, and did once,
but then he was out again—a wriggle, a flap—
that fish jumped out of my hat!—
and the line, gone loose, jerked, snapped, and he was back
in the water, the hook in him.

And he didn't turn into
a glimmering girl, like he did for
young Willie Yeats,
nor was he a Jesus, like for Lawrence;
he just drifted head down near the shallows,
huge, the huge hook in him.
And Louis and Phil came up in the other
canoe, and we got the flashlight on him,
and tried to get hold of him. But then, somehow,

we lost him, drifting about, he was not there
but gone somewhere deeper into the water,
every minute darker; my hook in him.

I hooked five or six snags after that, yelling
each time that each one was a fish, bigger
than the last. But I brought nothing living up.
And the other canoe went ghostly on the water,
silvery, like a dish with two quiet eggs in it;
and the pines were massed, dark, and stood and smelled
strong, like a bodyguard of dried fish.

3

Breathing, my brother in my house,
and breathing, his wife beside him.

Breathing, my brother in America,
his body in my bed, her body.

Their tent the color of the sun in my garden.
And they are riding West.

And both of us riding West, brother,
since we swam out of the father,

heading, six years apart,
the same way.

The dog stares at me, not knowing
why I have not fed him.
The cat crying to come in.

Whom we feed, sustain us.
Who need us, we keep breathing for.

I have seen you, at supper with friends,
put your hands to the guitar strings

and bring strong music out, seen you

sit and pick out

a tune on the piano,
on a friend's penny whistle.

To hold an instrument, to play.
To hold a pen, to write.

To do as little harm as possible
in the universe, to help

all traveling people, West, West;
you are not traveling alone,

not ever; we all go with you;
only the body stays behind.

4
When I stand on my island, a Napoleon,
one hand nailed to my chest,
the writing hand;

when I can only *stare*
at the ocean, at the birds
running and turning against the light . . .

When I am
the Illinois man and his kind,
"Talk to me, baby,"

the one with the knife inside, sometimes,
the one you may meet on your travels,
the one behind you in the line to get on the bus,

the one arranging a deal in a phone booth
as you drive past,
when I become that thing I sometimes become,

I will go into

the green of this visit, the green
you asked me to try to see

after my earlier, darker poems for you—
and this, the fourth one, darker
than I meant, since the man with the knife

swam into it—O when that killer
stands over our city, our sleeping and loving places,
tent, canoe, cabin of sweet people—

I will hear with your ears
the songs of the birds of the new world
that so quicken you, and look for

their wings that flame and flash—there!—
among the leaves and branches . . .

5

Too often I have wanted
to slip away, the hook in me,
to roll off the bed
and into the dark waters under it;
to drift, head down,
hide, hide, the hook in me;
to roll
in the wet ashes of the father,
wet with the death of the father,
and not try
to burn my way upward; the son, rising.

I swear to you now, I will survive,
rise up, and chant my way through these losses;

and you, you, brother, whatever that is,
same blood, you who swim
in the same waters,
you promise me to make *your* music too,

whatever the hurt;

O when we are almost only
mouth, when we are almost only a head
stuck on the pole of the body,
and the man says "Talk to me, baby,"
let's refuse him, brother, both, all of us,
and striking the spine like an instrument, inside,
like birds, with even the body broken,
our feathers fiery—there! there!—among
the leaves and branches, make
no sounds he will know;
like birds, my brother, birds of the new world, *sing*.

—*Michael Dennis Browne*

HIDDEN FALLS

for Matthew and Damian

Sentries stood here when the river was called
Mechesebe, Watapan Tancha:
Great river, body of rivers.

Two boys are running on a sandbar, kicking up spray
across the river.
It is a hundred in the sun.
Wind from the south.

Matthew and Damian are driving back to Indiana today.
A hundred years ago they would have gone this way
the way of the river.
It would be as if they were going down the river of sleep
and of time. The wind would be against them until they rounded
the bend to the left.

I am looking downstream into the heart
of the day. There have to be voices which belong to just the ground,
away from the landscape of a clock. I take three rocks which are like
three voices or three brothers.
I say, travel well, and throw them into the river.
Now we share the same water and go the same place.

                                        —*John Minczeski*

ATLANTIS

for Gary   Come Again (Hunter/ Garcia

      Come again   begging it
   wash of the organ   behind the cry
wash of rain   in the nose the one warm day, how long
till we hear it again, how much longer does winter
turn past us on those dark branches laced there
over the sun, and when the sun comes back
how is it going to look, How much longer
till we can smile together to see it rise

Some of these mornings it's been so easy
to see that continent rising in the West
easy as crossing the river, all of us brothers,
our arms around each other drinking beer in Kansas
where the sun went.   when the sun went
down   straind out our lives
that thin, I wonder if you knew, one red line
between the dark and the whole coming world.
            There is nothing to lose
The freight cuts that valley searching out the way north
with its light every night of the world and its horns
have lived in our sleep all our lives. How here in the north
this one pair of eyes keeps looking west across a river
    anchord   in all I have to lose, how the one
brother I've had can hang as you seemd to
onto some other bank, so much to lose, so daily torn at
by that massive stream.
Lord, there's an ocean out there.   and its wash
stands behind the rainstorm and stands in the clear light
of the acid the wash of electric sky   etcht
    with direction. A road to follow and a signpost
to leave behind. Some big hand pointing the way & flapping
in the wind. Arm round the shoulder, against the wind
Its wash. The arm of sleep around us both,
a mercy by now.   Some of these mornings the eyes
won't even open, arms around

so much the stream's washt down, & now
how to keep it here   neck lockt up
with the effort & the eyes narrowd.

        Gary those brothers
have all gone their ways and each one of us does that.
There are seasons so cold, turning our heads
to see each other so painful, we seem to have lost our way.
    How suddenly the wash of the train wheels
can show up in a dream;   the dream washt
behind the rotation of our daily lives like spring come again
The way you can lose
                        is not the way
        that it will come
& each of us with it   when we rise

                                —*Robert Ferguson*

UNWRITTEN LETTERS

for Jon Anderson and Gerald Orlen

This is one of those letters I meant to write
While shaving or walking the dog. It always begins
Dear Brother, or *Dear Friend*. When I was a child
I wrote things down and sewed words into sleeves,
Thoughts like clouds that changed when I watched them.
I buried them with the bottlecaps, the matchbooks,
In the backyard under the elm. I meant to dig them up.

Years later I think: Our lives change ceaselessly.
How much older we have grown. If I write this letter
This is how you'll remember me, the curtains shut,
The sun going down, the cells of my body stopped.
I must have been thinking of you, of all we've said
Or left unsaid; of all the things we meant
To do. There is nothing that I'm meant to say.

There's a mirror right above my desk. When I look up
There I am. The eyes drift. My face has lost
Its symmetry. The two halves live separately.
Is this what happens to people alone? I'm afraid
When you see me again, my face will suffer its parts
Unequally; one side will limp after the other,
Always the younger brother, unable to catch up.

When I look in the mirror, sometimes I see your face:
The eyes unfocused, settled within. The mouth says
Nothing now, content to wait. If we reached out
To touch one another, we would find the glass dark
And getting darker. To bring the two together
Requires patience, tact. My face is like the life I lead.
I meant to say, I'm doing fine. I can't describe it.

—Steven Orlen

MY BROTHER'S BRACES

My brother's braces, outgrown at night,
Fell in the dark like Cheyenne weapons,
Silvers of unmined power. Small
Chicken movements barked him handsome —
My mother smelled of lilacs and held him tight,
In the air he danced to no sound at all.

It was such lotions as made him laugh,
The nighttime moving captive on its knees,
That mounted my eyes till my blackfoot heart
Burst to a lilac roar.
My mother spoke in syllables too fair to hear;
My brother's metal braces spoke to me.

For what were my two good legs to think,
When lilac sold for fevers and a kiss?
Better the sky buckle and the moon shrink
Than that the purple-honeyed air
Drain cold, or the door close, lights
Island us forever with a mist.

And nowhere any stars. Legs gold,
I crashed among Klondikes, whipped trees,
Jigged in my irons till iron lay still.
For Queen Isabella, all these seas! —
Birds with their eyes closed let me see the Prince.
Across, his purple bed was drenched with bad dreams.

I think of my brother, grown straight and tall,
Walking in the daylight of that staunch town.
He has outgrown the cowboy, the cowhands that call,
And no street remembers that would lift us yet.
The lilac grows faint now, fainter as we touch;
Those braces will embrace me after death.

—Robert Hutchinson

BLUES FOR JIMMY

for Jimmy McGrath
killed June 1945

1.

(If it were evening on a dead man's watch,
Flowerfall, sundown, the light furled on the pane;
And the shutters going up on the windows of the twentieth century,
6 Post Mortem in the world of the dead—)

> The train was late. We waited among the others,
> All of us waiting for friends on the late train.
> Meanwhile the usual darkness, the usual stars,
> Allies of the light trust and homeless lovers.
> And then the train with its clanking mechanical fury.
> "Our will could neither turn it around nor stop it."
> Abrupt as history it violates the station—
> The knife, the dream, the contemporary terror.

(Midnight awakens on a dead man's watch:
The two exact figures in the million beds
Embrace like skeletons chained in other dreams,
In the world of the dead where love has no dominion.)

> "And then we took him to the funeral parlor,
> Half-way house, after the train came in."
> We found he had put on another face,
> The indifferent face of death, its brutality and pallor
> "And now at last, everyone is home?"
> All but you, brother. We left you there alone.

(The dead man's watch unlocks the naked morning,
And the day, already bandaging victories and wounds,
Assumes like Time the absolute stance of indifference,
On yesterday's sorrow setting its actual seal.)

84

Among the absorbing tenants of god's half-acre
We gave you back into the mundane chemistry.
The banker dug the grave, but the grave and gentle
Were part of the common plot. The priestly succor,
Scattering platitudes like wreaths of wilted flowers,
Drove in the coffin nails with god's own little hammer—
You are stapled still; and we are freed of onus.
Brother, te laudamus, hallowed be our shame.

(The shadow of noon—upon a dead man's watch—
Falls on the hours and mysteries; April, October
Darkening, and the forward and following centuries. The blind flyer
Locates himself on the map by that cone of silence.)

2.

Locates himself by that cone of silence,
But does not establish his private valence:
When the long grey hearse goes down the street
The driver is masked and his eyes are shut—

While confessing the dead man is his brother,
Only in dreams will admit the murder,
Accepting then what is always felt:
The massive implacable personal guilt.

Who refuses to be his brother's keeper
Must carry a knife and never sleep,
Defending himself at whatever cost
Against that blind importunate ghost.
Priest, banker, teacher or publican,
The mask of the irresponsible man
May hide from the masker his crimes of passion
But not the sin of his class position.

And what of the simple sensual man
Who only wants to be let alone,
With his horse and his hound and his house so fine,
A car and a girl and a voting machine?
Innocent Mr. and Mrs. Onan
Are dead before they have time to lie down.

The doorbell rings but they are away.
It is better to murder than deny.

The desperate laws of human motion
Deny innocence but permit salvation;
If we accept sentence before we are tried
We discover the crime our guilt had hid.
But the bourgeois, the saint, the two-gun man,
Who close the gates upon their dream,
Refuse to discover that of salvation
There is no private accumulation.

3.

The wind dies in the evening. Dust in the chill air
settles in thin strata, taking the light with it,
Dusk before dusk in the river hollows.
And westward light glamors the wide Missouri,
The foothills, the Rockies, the arc of the harping coast.
And then the brooding continental night.

When I was a child the long evenings of midsummer
Died slow and splendid on my bedroom windowpane,
And I went into sleep's magnetic landscape
With no fear of awakening in a country of nightmares.
It was easy then. You could let the light go—
Tomorrow was another day and days were all the same:
Pictures in a book you'd read, segments of sealed and certain time:
Easy to go back to the day before yesterday, the year before last.

But now it is impossible. The leaf is there, and the light,
Fixed in the photograph, but the happiness is lost in the album,
And your words are lost in the mind, and your voice in the years,
And your letters' improbable tongues trouble the attic darkness.

And this is the true nature of grief and the human condition:
That you are nowhere; that you are nowhere, nowhere,
Nowhere on the round earth, and nowhere in time,
And the days like doors close between us, lock us forever apart.

4.

Not where spring with its discontinued annuities
Fills birds' nests with watches, dyes the winds yellow,
Scatters on the night its little flowers of disenchantment
And a drunken alphabet like the memory of clocks.

Not where summer, at the mercury's Feast of Ascension,
Deploys in fields the scarecrows of remembrance;
Summer with the wheat, oil, bread, birth, honey and barley,
And a hypnotised regiment of weeping butterflies.

Not when fall reopens private wounds
To stain the leaves and split the stones in walls;
Opening the doors on the furniture of false enigmas
And a mechanical patter of crazy magicians.

Not when winter on the buried leaf
Erects its barricades of coal stoves and forgetfulness;
With the warmth indoors, talk, love, camaraderie,
And outside a blizzard of years and corpses.

The calendar dies upon a dead man's watch. He is nowhere,
Nowhere in time. And yet must be in Time.
And when the Fifth Season with its mass and personal ascensions—
Fire-birds rising from the burning towns of Negation
Orbit toward freedom—
Until then, brother, I will keep your watch.

5.

I will not deny you through grief,
Nor in the masks and horrors of the voodoo man
Nor sell you in a mass for the dead
Nor seven out and forget you
Nor evict your spirit with a charming rune.
Nor wear my guilt for a badge like a saint or a bourgeois poet.

I forgive myself of your death: Blind shadow of my necessity—
Per mea culpa—cast by a son of freedom
I climb the hill of your absolute rebellion.

I do not exorcise you: you walk through the dark wood before me.

Though I give your loves to the hours,
Your bones to the first four seasons
Your hope to the ironies
Your eyes to the hawks of heaven
Your blood is made part of the general-strike fund
Your courage is coined into the Revolution
Your spirit informs the winds of the Fifth Season.

Only the tick of a watch divides us.
The crime is to deny the union of opposites.
I make your death my watch, a coin of love and anger,
With your death on one side and mine on the other.
Locked on my wrist to remember us by.

—Thomas McGrath

IV. Poems For Friends & Lovers

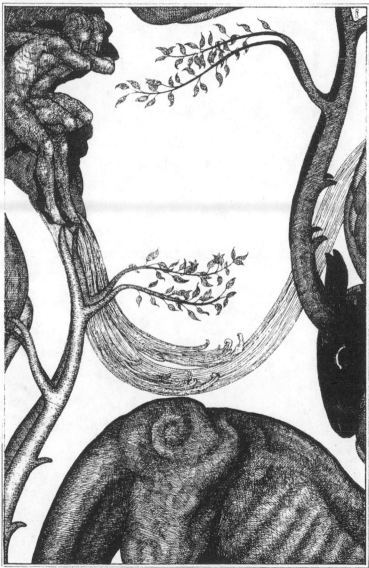

FRIENDS WITH STAGHORN.   1978   R. W. SCHOLES

I AM THE MAN WHO

I slouch down the dark, I am the dark
of a body; heavy-lidded, everywhere, flesh.
I am the blink that never opened
under the black hat at 3 a.m.: yes, I'll take you
to the station. But no smile
will open. I am the taken,
the fir-stained darkness stumbling
under your balcony. I am the unwatched silence
under your grey doves, inside your baskets,
blackening your crumpled scarves.
I am the shadow scarf under your throat,
rooting the flesh you would have opened too soon.
I am the dark insistence. You thought
I was a flute, I am the tenor sax, silver
on the outside, burnished a bruised apricot
inside the hole of my unblown music.
I am the man. I am there at North Beach,
bald, bent over the pool table, my fingers curled
around the cue. I am the man
in Seattle, blue-eyed, heavy under the ribs,
black raincoated, eating spicy shrimp soup at the market:
the waitress notices my hat, I tip
my body towards hers. She puts the green sauce of the hot peppers
over her eyes. I am the heat of a glance, I am the way
dusk crawls into darkness. I am
under your balcony, the rotten place
at the fallen petal's edge. I see how you see
the way men move: loose under the knees,
unexpectant, and slack: the way we enter doors,
heavily, suspicious of our own slow grace. It's me
being a man. I am the gait unfastened
from its purpose, I am the amble:
the fourth cross, the one
with no christ, no thieves,
the one the wind bends through all eternity.
I am the wind sulking under your balcony:
step down from your porch to my stories,

93

step down naked to my stories.

I am the fate, the dark streak of the communion rail:
kneel against me, put your thoughtless weight
to my grain. I am the certain root, blind,
erect, engraved in dirt. I am the surrounded;
I am the forbidden truth, I am the you
that always fought me. I am the fate.
I am the one who saw how the ocean takes what it wants.
I saw how the days lengthened slowly, and slowly
my light goes out to meet my darkness. Cliffs
of broken brown stone form along my edges.
I am the one you rode. I am the ridden one, the outflanked heart beat,
the one that was moved.
I am the one who was sung.
I am the lifted one, the falsetto
freed, finally at home with my joy. I am the man.

—James Moore

A COMMITMENT
for Steve Orlen

After I watched your face, behind its mask
Of talk, deaden, then grow animate,
Alternating light & dark as you bowed
& drew yourself erect under the lamplight
Of someone else's room in which we talked,
I was restored. Though in the minor
Darkness of my heart, where I'm most alone,
I wanted to take your masculine face
Between my hands & press for strength.
The skull, for me, is death & strength,
Merely objective in a world of sense.

Within a month you lost your wife & friend.
But not to death. I know their leaving
Had the appearance of a judgment on your life.
Because the friend was also mine & gone,
Because I loved your wife, in you or apart,
And because you wouldn't turn aside, I tilted
The lampshade down & drifted with you
On the edge of dark.

              I remembered an evening
With friends in a small boat on a lake.
It was September: the late afternoon light
& wine we drank warmed us to each other.
Our quietness then passed from the shadows
Of trees close to the water—it seemed
We had drifted out over a great emptiness,
Silent, held only by our composure . . .

I think, now, of those friends: I
Let them go. Really, only for the ease
Of letting go. Now when I visit & attend
Their lives, they are partly strange; I know
My hesitations seem to judge their house.

I wanted to say, as I watched you steady

Yourself in the dark, I was restored
By your bearing & openness to pain,
A commitment to what you had already lost.
Our talk was personal; I said it in another way.

But if all our losses are a form of death,
A mirror in which we see ourselves advance,
I believe in its terrible, empty reflection,
Its progress from judgment toward compassion.

—Jon Anderson

THE HUNGARIAN

If I waited till September
I could no longer walk on the bottom of the river.
I would be up to my waist in water,
fighting off gnats
and trying to find the stones with my soggy shoes.
By then the Hungarian would already be back in Europe,
telling his friends about the man he met in Pennsylvania
who spoke to him in German and told him about the
glaciers and the violent American poison.
—I could have kissed him goodbye, I knew him so well.
We walked up and down the mule path for two hours
with our hands behind us.
We bent down to pick up fish hooks and cigarette packs
as if we were walking through our own park.
We touched in each other one last loving time
the dream of justice we both had buried in our own rivers
like two gnostics who buried their city's statues
twenty feet down in the thick mud and the shadows
to keep them from greed and hatred,
to save them for the serious souls to come.

—Gerald Stern

AFTER HE SAID

"There's no such thing as human nature."
    —a Marxist, in conversation

Hubris was the word I wanted
and if I had found it
I could have strategically confessed
to my own: how, when I lived in New York

I believed I knew everything
but now know so much more.
But I said perversity was the first human
constant, and he frowned, this man I loved

for his nature, human and fine
and flawed. I wanted to say it's human nature
to create a politics so humane
it excludes half the world,

I wanted to say friendship, unlike history,
is what happens when two forces meet
and grow gentle—that's our history—
but I insisted on the perverse

and that wouldn't do,
he wasn't as perverse as I,
I should have named four or five
of the Seven Deadly Sins and said

when lust is culturally abolished
I'll be its guerilla priest
gathering followers in the hills.
I should have said, friend,

though it's human nature to forgive
as well as to never forgive,
we'll survive this argument,
it's human nature

to say No

to any self-assured Yes,
to make peace, to lie down happily
in strange beds.

—*Stephen Dunn*

SELF-INTERVIEWS

The shop teacher told you you'd end up
being a factory worker. But you died
before the dream could be fulfilled.
John, I've worked in a factory.
One morning, I was counting boxes of meat
in the freezer. This woman's face came before me.
It was peaceful and I've known other nights.

I desire teenage girls in Glencoe, autumn
afternoon drives along Sheridan Road.
Why am I so afraid of being alone?
Have I ever had an orgasm at the same
time that my lover has had an orgasm?
Sex is all and all too good to be true.
That's what the doctor said. That afternoon,
I didn't call you back from the dead
to cry for my life in the waiting room.

I make love to three women in nine days.
Señor Blues is what they call me.
Each time I plunge into my loneliness
I dream of a factory.
Twelve years ago we hitch-hiked
past the spot where you'd be underground.

We rode shoulder to shoulder on a bus
to have our pictures taken
by an older man living in a lonelier city.
I knew the dark thick skin of your body,
your uncircumsized penis, the tone of your voice
in a closeness as intimate as love.
And you used to think I was beautiful.

—*Peter Mladinic*

100

THE FIRST TIME

Sometimes I'm their first.
Sweet, sweet men.
I light candles, burn the best incense.
Make them think it's some kind of temple
and it rather is.

Like this guy who hauled parts for a living,
whatever the hell that means.
He was like caught light through glass
and so the candles and incense.
What would you do with a new colt?

He touched my body the way shadows fall
from an old subject he'd buried,
and he looked at me without fear.

Sweet guy.
So sweet I became really shy and hot,
so I had to move easy.
Wouldn't you?
What do you do when it's someone's first time?
I try to clean up my act.
Make it into a first rate number
where he knows he's been with someone.

We're bunglers when it's really good:
bow legs, pimply backs, scrawny chest hair,
full of mistakes and good intentions.
And it doesn't have anything to do with ladies.
They're fine too.
Just something between two men.

—*James L. White*

WRESTLERS

We begin on all fours,
six spikes driven into the mat.
I'm over him, chin sighting
along his back, left hand cupping
his elbow & right arm draped around
his waist like a girlfriend, palm
resting lightly on his belly.
We think about this awhile.
I'm as careful as a watchmaker
bending over a tiny spring.
I feel his leaning.
The ref waves his hand like
he's dropping a handkerchief.
My partner jumps away
to help him pick it up.
I gather my weight & his limbs
to me, think of Jesus & the lamb,
& cradle him in my arms.

—*S. Lewandowski*

SONG

O Joie
Why must I contain you
When I know I will be
With him in a day's spin

O Joie
To hear him breathe again
And to know those intimacies
That bodies do do together

O Joie
To lay near him again
So close that his presence
Will lie inside my body

O Joie
Why must I contain you
When I know I will be
A swallow at a worm

O Joie
I am having a civil war
With my selves, the hermetic
Against the experientialist

O Joie
Why must I contain you
Who have been hearing
All the swallows in One Song

—Paul Mariah
August 18, 1973
San Francisco

UNBRIDLING OUR HORSES

Unbridling our horses
   my hands were numb
   from the cold
   and the long ride home
We had sung Indian
   songs
   on the way
   I could tell in your
   voice that you were
   lonesome
   That's why I brushed
   the snow from your
   hair
   spoke no words except
   in singing and
   watched the white
   whirlwinds dancing
   at our feet
As I was building up
   the fire
   I looked to see
   you coming from
   the barn staring
   at the ground then
   looking up to let
the snow melt on your cheeks
Before you hit the porch
   I heard you throwing up
   all that beer
Already I was thinking
   about summer—
   pow-wows and rodeos,
   fry bread cooking
   around the camps
When you came in half
   smiling I could
   tell you felt better
   so I lit you a
   cigarette and warmed up
   some left over
   chili

Pinon flames leaped into
   the soot covered
   chimney
   mesmerizing us until
   the first light of
   dawn
Hearing my name called
   I remember only
   the wind whining
   causing the logs to
   creak
   and the warm hand
   touching my face
The storm had nearly
   cleared
   as you rode off
   glancing towards
the ghost-like mountains
   I almost missed
   your wave
The house was really
   quiet now
   I warmed up the
   coffee and cut out
   a new pair of
   moccasins
In the late day
   I broke up flecks
   of hay to snorts
   of frozen breath
and thought of
   following your trail
but I knew that
   you had left no
   trail
   that the end of the
   long winter would
   uncover the
   loneliness
and we would be
   dancing together
   somewhere in the
summer . . . .
            Barney Bush

THE STONES
for David Ignatow

Your words arrive
on wings of a bird of omen,
feathers shining, fiery silk in the sun.

In my pocket are stones,
their weight wears the cloth threadbare
but nothing falls through.
I hold to them hour on hour,
secrets at my fingertips,
a rosary of tears, wishes,
and the slow death by which we live.

This stumping of roads leads on,
the ground softens, our feet drag, then sink,
we become where we are.

Not yet.
Today the sky clears off haze and clouds
and burns a blue flame we could walk under
together a long time.

Listen: the grass here is still green,
the elms just turning.
Step out in the landscape;
before it rains we will plant our stones.

—*Ralph J. Mills, Jr.*

SONG FOR MEETING A FRIEND
(in the Nahua mode)

Friend—
    your eyes are perforated mirrors;
    in them I see myself & beyond—
    (your heart holds
        flowers
        feathers
        pieces of jade)
Your voice is full
    of the smell of flowers
    of the sound of song.
On your feet is the dust
    of paths leading thru darkness
    of paths leading to light.

We have traveled long distances;
our hands have longed to touch.

    I recognize you:
        your face, your heart.

Brother:
    for what has been
            thanks
    for what is
            joy
    for what will be
            yes.

—*Rafael Jesús González*

MAKING LOVE TO MYSELF

When I do it, I remember how it was with us,
then my hands remember too,
and you're with me again just the way it was.

After work when you'd come in and
turn the t.v. off and sit on the edge of the bed,
filling the room with gasoline smell from your overalls,
trying not to wake me which you always did
and I'd breathe out long and say:
"Hi Jess, you tired baby?"
You'd say not so bad and rub my belly,
not after me really, just being sweet,
and I'd always die a little from loving you.
I always thought I'd die a little
because you smelt like burnt leaves or wood smoke.

We were poor as Job's turkey and lived really well:
the food, a few movies, good dope, lots of talk,
lots of you and me trying on each other's skin.

What a sweet gift this is,
done with my memory, my cock and hands.

I wake up wondering if I should fix
coffee for us before work,
almost thinking you're here again,
almost seeing your work jacket on the chair.

I wonder if you remember what
we promised when you took the job in Laramie?
Our way of staying with each other.
We promised there'd always be times
when the sky was perfectly lucid,
that we could remember each other through that.

You could remember me at my work table
or the all night diners,
that we'd never call or write.

I have to stop here Jess.
I just have to stop here.

—James L. White

NIGHT REGRESSION POEM

I don't know
who you are
yet
you are
weakening me

I don't sleep
and once under
naked
you drift in
and poise on my
chest and blow
breath on my
hair

the door groans
letting you in
the clock
skips
and the furnace
rattles breaking
chains

I pretend
I'm a child
cradled
in sweat, I
want you to say
whether
you are innocent
I want to sleep
I want you to
take me

—Robert Peters

SONG
after Moses Ibn Ezra

Circumstance has estranged my friend.
He has bolted the door
but I will enter the portal
and knock
          despite my enemies.
I will shatter locks with words.
I will break bolts with my songs
and will persuade myself
that nettles are sprigs of balsam.
I will dance and shout to their bitter juice
as if I were drunk on wine
and humble myself
and pretend that hell stream is icy
if it will get me through the darkness
                        into his light.

Go now, my song,
take this message to my beloved,
for song is a faithful messenger.

—Carl Rakosi

111

CONTRIBUTORS

JON ANDERSON lives in Tucson, Arizona where he teaches in the M. F. A. program at the University of Arizona. His latest book is *In Sepia* (University of Pittsburgh Press).

ROBERT BLY, born in 1926, has received numerous awards for his poetry and translations. He is the founder of The Seventies Press and the creator of the annual "Conference on The Great Mother and The New Father." He is completing an anthology of ecology poems for the Sierra Club to be called *News of the Universe*. Harper & Row will publish his newest collection of poems this summer entitled *This Tree Will Be Here For A Thousand Years*.

MICHAEL DENNIS BROWNE's poem, "Talk To Me, Baby," was included in the 3rd Annual Pushcart Prize anthology and appears in his second collection of poetry, *The Sun Fetcher*, published by Carnegie-Mellon University Press. He teaches at the University of Minnesota.

BARNEY BUSH was presented with the Grand Award for poetry at the Scottsdale National Indian Arts Exposition 1976, in Arizona. He has been the subject of educational tv documentaries and his work has appeared in *Scree, Indian America, Akwesasne Notes,* and in numerous environmental magazines. His new book of poems is called *My Horse and A Jukebox*.

ALVARO CARDONA-HINE lives in Saint Paul, Minnesota. His last three books are all from Red Hill Press: *Words on Paper, Two Elegies,* and translations of Vallejo's *Spain, Let This Cup Pass From Me*.

PAUL CARROLL was born 1927 in Chicago. He is Professor of English and former Chairman of the Program for Writers, University of Illinois at Chicago Circle. He was poetry editor of *Chicago Review*, 1957-1959 and editor and publisher of *Big Table*, 1959-1961. His books include *Odes* (1968), *The Poem in Its Skin* (1968), and *The Luke Poems* (1971). His most recent publication is *New and Selected Poems* (Yellow Press, 1978).

HENRY COMBELLICK lives in Tucson, Arizona. He has done graduate work at the University of Montana and Brown University. His poems have been published in *Poetry Now, Boston Phoenix, Pebble, Slackwater Review,* and other magazines.

PHILIP DACEY lives and teaches in Cottonwood, Minnesota. His most recent collections of poetry are *How I Escaped From The Labyrinth and Other Poems* (Carnegie-Mellon University Press, 1977) and *The Condom Poems* (Ox Head Press, 1979).

JOSEPH P. DARCY is presently finishing his B.A. degree at the State University of New York at Buffalo. His poetry will appear in the anthology *In Logan's Room* (BOA Editions) later this year. "Beyond the Window" is his first published poem. Thanks to John Logan for recommending his work.

JAMES DICKEY, born in 1923, presently lives in Columbia, South Carolina. He has received the National Book Award for Poetry (1966) and is the author of several poetry collections including *Drowning With Others, Helmets,* and *Buckdancer's Choice*.

113

STEPHEN DUNN currently teaches at Stockton State College in New Jersey. He has published three collections of poetry, the most recent being *A Circus of Needs* (Carnegie-Mellon University Press, 1978).

MICK FEDULLO holds degrees from Goddard College and the University of Iowa and has published poems in *Chicago Review, Antaeus, Iowa Review,* and *Choomia.* Porch Publications will publish a collection of his work entitled *In My Brother's House.* He lives in Tucson, Arizona.

DAVID J. FEELA presently lives in Maple Lake, Minnesota. He works for the St. Cloud public library as a clerk-typist and offset printer. His work has appeared in *Studio One.*

ROBERT FERGUSON was born in St. Joseph, Missouri, and now lives in St. Paul, Minnesota. *The River Road* was published in 1978 by Truck Press.

SID GERSHGOREN lives in St. Paul, Minnesota. His first book of poems, *Negative Space,* was published in 1975 by Red Hill Press. A new book of poems, *But Listen The Shout Comes Back To Me,* is in preparation for publication. Recent work in *Harbinger* magazine.

RAFAEL JESÚS GONZÁLEZ was born in El Paso, Texas and currently teaches Literature and Creative Writing at Laney College, Oakland, California. His collection of poems, *El Hacedor de Juegos/The Maker of Games,* was published in 1978 by Casa Editorial.

DONALD HALL has recently published *Remembering Poets* (memoirs of Dylan Thomas, Frost, Eliot, and Pound) and *Kicking the Leaves* (new poems), both from Harper & Row. A new book, *Goatfoot Milktongue Twinbird,* is from the University of Michigan Press.

ROBERT HUTCHINSON's books of poetry include *The Kitchen Dance* and, from Eakins Press, *Standing Still While Traffic Moves About Me* (1971). His stories have appeared in *Harper's* and other places, and he is at work on a novel, *The Wheat Stone.* Born in Hutchinson, Kansas, he lives and works in New York City. He is a younger brother.

DAVID IGNATOW's recent honors include the Bollingen Prize (1977) and a Wallace Stevens Fellowship at Yale University (1977). His tenth book of poetry, *Tread the Dark,* was published in 1977.

WILLIAM KLOEFKORN writes "I'm married and have two sons and two daughters. The poem that represents me in this anthology is one I wrote shortly after my older son was married. I don't let go of things easily. He now has a daughter that will be two years old when this book appears, and, totally unlike the other granddaughters, this one is both bright and beautiful. Even so, I somehow expect my son to return the football one of these days, though I realize that he can't stay. I have five collections of poetry published and two more scheduled for publication this year." He lives in Lincoln, Nebraska.

RONALD KOERTGE is the author of seven books of poetry and has recently had a novel accepted by W.W. Norton for publication. He lives in South Pasadena, California.

114

TED KOOSER works as an insurance underwriter in Lincoln, Nebraska and edits and publishes Windflower Press books. He has two book-length collections in print, *A local habitation & a name* (Solo Press,1974), and *Not Coming To Be Barked At* (Pentagram Press, 1976). His most recent book is *Hatcher*, a novel in pictures.

NORBERT KRAPF was born in Jasper, Indiana and presently teaches at the C. W.Post Center of Long Island University. A chapbook of poems, *The Playfair Book of Hours* appeared in 1976 (Ally Press), and *Finding the Grain*, a collection of pioneer journals, Franconian folktales and poems was published in 1977 by the Dubois County Historical Society. Two more chapbooks, *The Darkening Green* (Rook Press) and *Arriving on Paumanok* (Street Press) will appear in 1979.

GREG KUZMA lives in Crete, Nebraska where he runs The Best Cellar Press. Harry Duncan's Abattoir Editions will publish his long poem for his brother Jeff, tentatively entitled *Poem For My Brother*.

PHILIP LEVINE was Poet-in-Residence at the National University of Australia, Canberra, during the summer, 1978. He taught at Vassar during winter, 1979. He has two books due from Atheneum this spring, *Ashes* and *7 Years From Somewhere*. He lives in Fresno, California with his wife and sons and teaches at California State University.

STEPHEN LEWANDOWSKI used to wrestle in the 127 pound class. His first full-length collection of poems, *Inside & Out*, appeared this year from Crossing Press.

GERALD LOCKLIN teaches at California State University at Long Beach and has books forthcoming this spring including *The First Time I Saw Spring* (a novel, New Earth Books), and *Men and Women* (poems, Northwoods Press).

JOHN LOGAN is Professor of English at the State University of New York at Buffalo. He has published seven books of poetry. Recent poems appear in *Paris Review* and *Poetry*. He is the founder and co-editor of *Choice*, a magazine of poetry and graphics.

PAUL MARIAH's newest book is *This Light Will Spread*: Selected Poems 1960-1975 from ManRoot Press which he operates in South San Francisco, California.

KEN McCULLOUGH has published three books of poetry: *The Easy Wreckage* (1971), *Migrations* (1973), and *Creosote* (1976). He received an NEA Fellowship in 1974. He is currently Writer-in-Residence with the South Carolina Educational TV Network.

THOMAS McGRATH was born in North Dakota and educated at the University of North Dakota, Louisiana State University, and New College, Oxford University where he was a Rhodes Scholar. He has held the Amy Lowell Travelling Poetry Scholarship, and was awarded a Guggenheim and Bush Foundation Fellowship. He is the author of the epic poem *Letter to An Imaginary Friend*, *The Movie at the End of the World* (both from Swallow Press), *Open Songs* (Uzzano Press) and *letters to tomasito* (Holy Cow! Press, 1977). He presently lives in Moorhead, Minnesota and teaches at Moorhead State.

RALPH J. MILLS, JR. teaches at the University of Illinois at Chicago Circle. His most recent books include *Night Road/Poems* (Rook Press, 1978), and *Living With Distance* (poems, BOA Editions, 1979). He is currently editing the selected essays and interviews of David Ignatow for the University of Michigan's "Poets on Poetry" Series.

JOHN MINCZESKI lives and teaches in St. Paul, Minnesota. His first collection of poems will be published this spring by New Rivers Press. He has taught in the Twin Cities Poets-in-the-Schools program and has worked in the ESAA Special Arts Project in Community Education in St. Paul.

PETER MLADINIC is a native of New Jersey and presently lives in Minneapolis where he works for The Loft—A Place for Literature and the Arts.

JAMES MOORE's most recent book of poems is *What The Bird Sees* (Momentum Press). He currently lives in St. Paul where he is completing a mystery novel.

DAVID MURA is a Ph.D. candidate in English at the University of Minnesota. He has published in various little magazines and was the 1978 co-winner of the Academy of American Poets' Prize at the University of Minnesota.

STEVEN ORLEN's most recent book is *Permission To Speak* (Wesleyan University Press). He teaches creative writing in the English Department at the University of Arizona in Tucson.

BILL PAULY currently teaches at Loras College in Dubuque, Iowa. He has written two chapbooks of haiku, *Wind The Clock By Bittersweet* and *Time From His Bones*.

ROBERT PETERS teaches at the University of California, Irvine, specializing in Victorian Literature and contemporary poetry. He has published fourteen books of poetry in the last ten years including *Gauguin's Chair*: Selected Poems (Crossing Press, 1977), *Holy Cow*: Parable Poems (Red Hill Press, 1974), *Cool Zebras of Light* (Christopher's Books, 1974), *The Sow's Head & Other Poems* (Wayne State University Press, 1968) and *Songs for a Son* (W. W. Norton, 1967).

CARL RAKOSI's poems first appeared in *The Little Review* and in Ezra Pound's *The Exile* in the 1920's. In the early 1930's he was associated briefly with the Objectivists. His recent poetry collections include *Ere-Voice* (New Directions, 1971), *Ex Cranium, Night* (Black Sparrow Press, 1975) and *My Experiences in Parnassus* (Black Sparrow Press, 1977). A former resident of Minneapolis, he recently moved to San Francisco.

GEORGE ROBERTS lives in Minneapolis. His second chapbook, *night visits to a wolf's howl*, is forthcoming from Oyster Press.

VERN RUTSALA's recent publications include *The Journey Begins* (University of Georgia Press), *Paragraphs* (Wesleyan), and *The New Life* (Trask House). He lives in Portland, Oregon where he teaches at Lewis and Clark College.

REG SANER lives in Boulder, Colorado where he teaches, skiis, and hikes. Recent work appears in *A Geography of Poets*, ed. by Edward Field (Bantam Books, 1979).

116

RICHARD SHELTON's most recent book, *The Bus to Veracruz* (University of Pittsburgh Press), has been nominated for both a Pulitzer Prize and a National Book Award. His other books published by the same press are *The Tattooed Desert*, *Of All The Dirty Words*, and *You Can't Have Everything*. He teaches in the writing program at the University of Arizona and directs Writer's Workshops in two Arizona prisons.

MORTY SKLAR was born in New York City, 1935 and moved to Iowa City in 1971, where he became involved in the community of poets there, the *Actualists*. In 1975 he began *The Spirit That Moves Us* magazine, and recently put out the 10th issue. A collection of his own poetry, *The Night We Stood Up For Our Rights*, is from Toothpaste Press (1977). Also in 1977, he co-edited (with Darrell Gray) and published *The Actualist Anthology*. Forthcoming at the end of 1979, from his The Spirit That Moves Us Press, is *Editors' Choice: Literature & Graphics from the United States Small Press, 1965-1977*, co-edited by him and Jim Mulac. He is finishing a novel, *Getting Up*. Poems and sections of his novel recently appeared in *New Letters*, *Greenfield Review*, and *Rockbottom*.

ARTHUR SMITH's poems, interviews, and reviews have appeared in *Chicago Review*, *Stand* (England), *The Ohio Review*, *The Ardis Anthology of New American Poetry*, and many other journals. He currently teaches and is in the doctoral program at Ohio University.

GARY SNYDER was born in 1930 in San Francisco and was educated at Reed, Berkeley, Indiana, and a Japanese Zen monastery. He has worked as a logger, forest ranger, and a seaman. Included among his many books is *Turtle Island* (New Directions, 1974) which won the Pulitzer Prize for Poetry in 1975.

WILLIAM STAFFORD's recent collection of poems, *Stories That Could Be True*: New and Collected Poems, was published by Harper & Row in 1977. A prose book, *Writing the Australian Crawl*: Views on the Writer's Vocation, was published in 1978 by the University of Michigan Press.

GERALD STERN lives in Raubsville, Pennsylvania. He is the author of *Rejoicings* (Fiddlehead Poetry Books) and *Lucky Life* (Houghton Mifflin) which won the Lamont Poetry Award for 1977. A column of his, called "Notes from the River," appears regularly in *American Poetry Review*.

CHARLES WATERMAN is the author of two collections of poetry: *The Place* (Minnesota Writer's Publishing House) and *Talking Animals* (*Northeast*/Juniper Books). He lives in LeCenter, Minnesota with his wife Cary and their children.

JAMES L. WHITE presently lives in Minneapolis where he was recently awarded the 1978 Bush Foundation Fellowship for Poetry. He has published three books of poems: *Divorce Proceedings* (University of South Dakota Press, 1972), *A Crow's Story of Deer* (Capra Press, 1974), and *The Del Rio Hotel* (Territorial Press, 1975).

DAVID WOJAHN teaches English at the University of Arizona, where he is working on an M.F.A. His poems have appeared in *Dacotah Territory*, *The Iowa Review*, *Porch*, and *The Chariton Review*. He also teaches in the Poetry-in-the-Schools program for the Arizona Commission of the Arts.

CHARLES WRIGHT is the author of *The Grave of the Right Hand, Hard Freight, Bloodlines*, and *China Trace*. He presently lives in Laguna Beach, California. His latest book is *The Storm* (Field Editions) — translations of Eugenio Montale.

JAMES WRIGHT was born in Martin's Ferry, Ohio, in 1927, and was educated at Kenyon College and the University of Washington-Seattle. He is presently an English teacher at Hunter College in New York City. His work has received many honors including the Pulitzer Prize in 1972 for his *Collected Poems*.

The artist, RANDALL W. SCHOLES, was raised in the Dakotas and Minnesota. He has illustrated over ten books of poetry including *25 Minnesota Poets* (1 & 2) and has been published in innumerable magazines and journals. He is currently working as a freelance artist with the Saint Paul Pioneer Press.

The editor, JIM PERLMAN, was born and raised in Minneapolis, Minnesota. He was co-founder and co-editor of a number of little magazines including *One* (University of Minnesota), *Window Rock* (University of Arizona) and *Moons and Lion Tailes*. He is presently completing graduate work at the University of Iowa.